Soil Magic

Written by Tulani Thomas

Illustrated by Seitu Hayden

To: Sunny
Thanks for the
support.
small Acts Big Impacts

This book is dedicated to my heartbeats and village of love.

Catalog-in-Publication Data has been applied for and may be obtained from the Library of Congress.
ISBN 978-0-9846012-2-6
Text and Illustrations copyright © 2023 TuTu's Green World LLC
Illustrations and book design by Seitu Hayden

"Yuck! The Greenville Town Dump smells horrible"
TuTu said to Jennifer and Bryce
as they walked home from school.
Jennifer and Bryce are her best friends.

Greenville
Town Dump

The trio called themselves the Green Crew,
helping TuTu with her big green ideas.
"I can't wait until tomorrow's meeting.
Mayor Green will let me share my
composting idea!" TuTu remarked.
"We hope so," Jennifer and Bryce said.
That's all TuTu talked about for many weeks.

On Saturday morning, all of the residents of Greenville were at the Town Hall Meeting.

"Yuck! The Town Dump stinks
and looks horrible!"
the residents complained.

Mayor Green agreed. "TuTu, you talked about composting. Can you please share that concept with all of us?

5

"When we compost, we collect stale food, paper napkins, and yard waste. After some time, it becomes food for our plants and flowers. It's awesome!" TuTu said with excitement.

"The compost will become soil magic because of the many nutrients it adds to the soil."

"The compost or soil magic, will be used for our town gardens and parks.

cardboard
paper towels

meat

veggie
and
fruit
scraps

bones

coffee
grounds and
tea bags

leaves and
yard waste

OK

COMPOST

We'll have larger flowers and sweeter fruit at the farmer's market."

greasy containers

styrofoam

charcoal

plastic

metal

dairy products

MILK

fat/oils

OIL

coated paper

animal waste

KITTY LITTER

COMPOST

NOT OK

"We will post flyers in the post office, bakery, and library. They will explain the days the town empties the bins," TuTu continued. "We won't hand out flyers today, because it adds more trash," she explained with a wink and smile.

14

"Hooray!" everyone cheered, and the Green Crew went to work. They posted the flyers and dropped off bins. Everything went according to plan.

FREE
COMPOST
BINS

CITY
PICK-UP
EVERY
FRIDAY

COMPOST

The following week, the dump had less waste,
but the town was still smelly.
"My goodness, what is that odor?"
wondered Bryce.

The Green Crew rode around the neighborhood.
They couldn't believe their eyes.
The bins had not been emptied!
Their flyers were torn down and the
pick-up day was changed!

"Who would do such vandalism?!" exclaimed Jennifer, as Aaron and his friends rode away quickly. Aaron was annoyed that the Green Crew was getting all the attention.

TuTu immediately visited Mayor Green
at Town Hall to explain what happened.
"Our flyers listed the compost pick-up day;
many flyers were torn down
and the pick-up day was changed
on others. People didn't know
when to put their bins out for pick-up."

"Maybe we can send a text alert to everyone, to give the correct pick-up day?" TuTu suggested.

Strolling the neighborhood, TuTu
noticed many bins had toppled over.
Trash covered the streets.
TuTu and her crew cleaned up the
mess and stood the bins upright.
"How did these bins get
knocked over?" mused TuTu.
"Is it the wind?"

One day compost pick-up
discovered a surprise.
They found the culprits, at last!

Aaron and his friends were embarrassed and apologized. They decided to help the Green Crew rather than try to destroy their composting plan.

COMPOST

Over the next few weeks,
the compost pick-ups went as planned.
The dump had less trash, and the
horrible smell was gone.

TuTu and the Green Crew, with the help of Aaron and his friends made sure the compost was used in Greenville's gardens and parks. The compost became soil magic and everything blossomed.

Types of Composting

Community Composting is when a group of people in a neighborhood work together to compost and bring their compost to a central composting facility to be shared in the community gardens or green spaces.

Backyard Composting is done in your own backyard where you collect organic waste like fruit peels, vegetable scraps, and leaves, and put them in a compost pile or bin.

Worm Composting or **Vermicomposting** is a special type of composting where you create a worm bin and add food scraps and other organic materials. The worms eat the waste and turn it into nutrient-rich worm compost. The worms are little compost superheroes working in the bin!

Indoor Composting is when you compost inside your house or classroom and you collect organic waste like fruit peels, vegetable scraps, and leaves, in a special compost bin or container.

Schoolyard Composting is done at school where students and teachers collect food scraps from the cafeteria or classroom and put them in a compost bin with other organic materials like leaves or grass clippings. The waste turns into compost that is used in the school garden or shared with the local community.

Printed in the USA
CPSIA information can be obtained
at www.ICGtesting.com
CBHW040100170724
11649CB00008BA/13